bringing up baby

wild animal families

bringi

baby

PUBLISHING

Discovery Channel Publishing

Crown Publishers, Inc., New York

ng up

wild animal families

By Kit Carlson

Illustrated by Anders Wenngren

Published by Crown Publishers, Inc., a Random House company, 201 East 50th Street, New York, New York 10022

http://www.randomhouse.com/

CROWN is a trademark of Crown Publishers, Inc.

Printed in the United States of America

Library of Congress Cataloging-in-Publication Data
Carlson, Kit.
Bringing up baby: wild animal families / by Kit Carlson; illustrated by Anders Wenngren.
        p.   cm.
Includes index.
Summary: A collection of facts about how many different animals behave in relation to courtship, mating, and caring for offspring.

1. Familial behavior in animals—Juvenile literature.
[1. Familial behavior in animals. 2. Animals—Habits and behavior. 3. Animals—Miscellanea.] I. Wenngren, Anders, ill. II. Title.
QL761.5.C37   1998
591.56'3—dc21   97-42898

ISBN   0-517-80007-1 (paperback)
             0-517-80008-X (lib. bdg.)

Inspired by Animal Planet, the cable television network from the people who bring you the Discovery Channel. For more information about Animal Planet's availability on your basic channel line-up, contact your cable or satellite company and visit our web site at *www.animal.discovery.com.*

*For Andrew and Katie
and all the half-grown wild things*

Art Director: David Cullen Whitmore
Design: Studio A

Photo Credits: All photographs supplied by Bruce Coleman, Inc.

Credits from left to right are separated by semicolons, from top to bottom by dashes.

Cover: Mark Newman; Leonard Rue, Jr. 6, 7: F. Aberham. 9: Laura Riley. 10: M. P. Kahl. 12: Clem Haagnero. 14: Ron & Valerie Taylor. 17: Karl Ammann. 18, 19: Tom Brakefield. 20: Bob & Clara Calhoun. 22: Francisco Erize. 23: Leonard Lee Rue III. 24: Joe & Carol McDonald. 25: John Flannery—Leonard Lee Rue III. 26: Erwin & Peggy Bauer. 27: Joe McDonald—Karl & Kay Ammann. 28: Charles G. Summers Jr.—Joe McDonald. 29: Leonard Lee Rue III. 30: Laura Riley—Jeff Foott. 31: Jen & Des Bartlett. 32: Norman Owen Tomalin. 33: Kim Taylor. 34: Norman Myers. 36, 37: Wayne Lankinen. 39: David Madison. 40: Norman Owen Tomalin. 42: Dotte Larse. 45: Joe & Carol McDonald. 46: Laura Riley. 49: Ed. R. Degginger. 51: Kim Taylor. 53: Phil Degginger. 54, 55: Jen & Des Bartlett. 56: Wendell Matzen. 58: R. Kopfle. 60: Peter Davey. 63: Jen & Des Bartlett. Back Cover: Dotte Larse.

Contents

we are fam
how animals live together

Pledge of Allegiance

When a wolf pack reunites—whether after a hunt or just a midafternoon nap—all the members greet the alpha (dominant) wolves, licking and nuzzling their faces. By touching and sniffing the alpha male and female, the pack shows its loyalty to the leaders, while reminding themselves that they're all members of the same pack.

ily

One Big Happy Family

A Tail of Two Titis
South American titi monkeys like to "hold tails" when they sit together. Mom and dad titis are especially fond of tail twining, but any two family members can be found, tail wrapped in tail, whether awake or asleep.

▼ Happy Birthday
The whole family gathers around to watch when new beavers are born—the father, two older beavers on the verge of moving out, and two yearlings. They'll all be standing by Mom as the new siblings slip out onto the floor of the beaver lodge.

Birds of a Feather Flock Together
Canada geese not only mate for life, they also stick close to their families. That big honking V that you see flying overhead is probably a collection of close relatives—sisters, brothers, cousins, aunts, and uncles—heading off in one family flock.

Monkey Sing, Monkey Do
Every morning, the jungles of southeast Asia ring with the almost operatic duets of gibbons in love. Mother and father gibbons greet the dawn with a song to reinforce their own bond and to warn other gibbons away from their territory.

Stand by Me
Zebras don't rush off when they're on the move—the whole herd travels at the pace of the slowest member. And they don't leave anyone behind. If even one zebra gets lost, the herd's stallion will search, calling with a barking bray until the missing member of his herd is found.

▼ Family Reunion

After the rainy season, as many as 2,000 African elephants assemble on the savanna, every elephant related to all the others, even if only distantly. These gatherings are annual reunions of kinship groups—bands of related elephants living in the same area—that meet to reestablish their bonds while feasting on new leaves and grass. The elephants notify others of their location using rumblings that are too low for humans to hear but that can carry for miles.

WHAT'S YOUR FAMILY NAME?

A group of	Is called a
Killer whales	pod
Prairie dogs	coterie
Lions	pride
Hippopotamuses	school
Baboons	troop
Warthogs	sounder
Wildebeests	herd

To Serve and Protect

Bringing Up the Rear

Male lions don't seem to do much—just lie around and wait for the lionesses to bring back supper. But they do play good defense. They protect the hunting territory against invading lions, and they also act as a rear guard when the pride is on the move, protecting the cubs from predators.

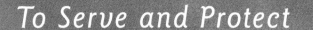

Gather the Troops!

When predators threaten young musk oxen, the adults make a tight circle around the calves, facing outward to ward off danger with their sharp, curving horns.

Pick Your Battles

Mole-like elephant shrews don't tolerate invaders in their burrows. They fight them off according to gender—the female shrew will attack other females, and the male will take on invading males.

There's Safety in Numbers

One hundred thousand strong, a colony of Adélie penguins can easily defend its chicks against hungry skuas. If these seabirds attack by air, thousands of upturned penguin beaks scream at them. If a skua tries to waddle into the colony on foot, storming penguins drive it off, rolling their eyes and snapping their beaks.

Don't Mess with These Mothers

Eland mothers join forces to defend their calves against all attackers. These feisty antelopes will fight anything that approaches in a threatening manner, including warthogs, baboons, and birds. Herds of female elands have even been seen chasing lions and cheetahs away from their babies.

▼ Duck!

If an eider duckling is threatened by a dive-bombing gull, the nearest adult eider duck may dive, grab the duckling by the feet, and drag it down to the safety of deep water.

Take Cover
Meerkats often leave their babies in the care of a few "aunties," related females who babysit while the parents go out in search of food. When a hawk soars over a meerkat colony, those aunties fling themselves over the young meerkats, even though the babies aren't their own.

Adopt-a-Dog

When an African wild dog mother died, the rest of the pack rallied around to care for the five-week-old pups. These wild dogs—all males—successfully raised the pups to adulthood.

Well, I'll Be a Monkey's Uncle

Among savanna baboons, a male may hang out around a certain female, acting as an "uncle" to her children. If those babies get rough treatment from other baboons, the uncle throws his weight around. He'll step right in, protecting them from harm while looking impressive to the female, who may decide to become his mate.

Bridge to Safety

Mother howler monkeys will make a bridge of their bodies, stretching out between two trees so their babies can cross the wide divide safely.

▼ Good Neighbors

If one bluebird parent dies, other bluebirds will help the remaining parent raise the chicks. The neighbor birds will bring insects to be sure the babies get fed and fledged, just as people bring casseroles to help out families in need.

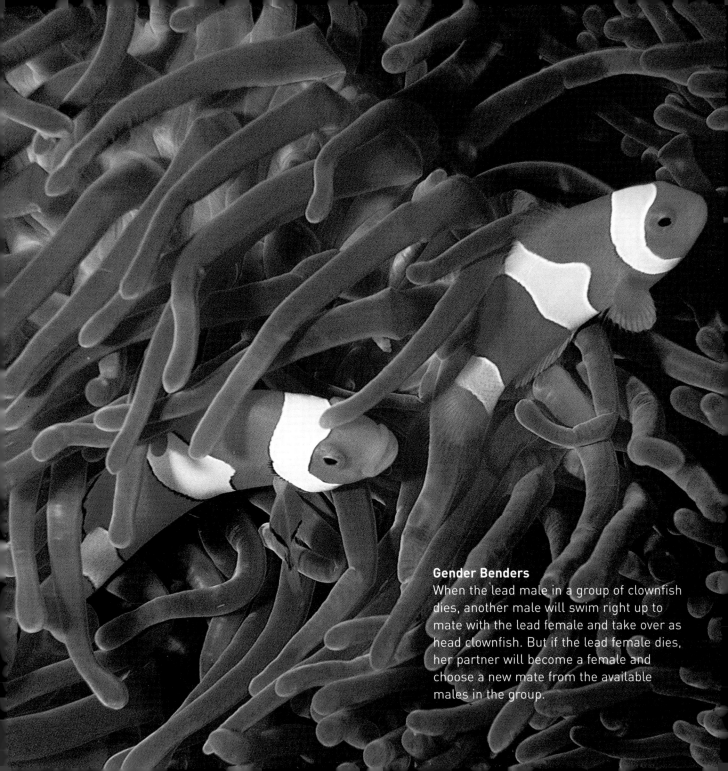

Gender Benders
When the lead male in a group of clownfish dies, another male will swim right up to mate with the lead female and take over as head clownfish. But if the lead female dies, her partner will become a female and choose a new mate from the available males in the group.

Under Her Thumb

In their underground warren, naked mole-rats must yield to their queen. She is the only female who may reproduce, and her children must dig and defend the tunnels. The queen even supplies a form of birth control: the worker mole-rats bathe daily in her urine. It contains a chemical that prevents them from reproducing.

Gentle Giant

With huge canine teeth and strength ten times that of a football player, a silverback gorilla doesn't have any problem keeping his troop of up to 20 apes in line. Just a grunt or a growl and everyone yields. Yet this same terrifying animal indulges his young, letting them climb and chase all over him for hours.

▶ Second-Class Citizen

When a female paper wasp queen can't get her act together to form her own colony, she moves into a nest with a more successful queen. Whenever this squatter queen gets the chance, she tries to lay her own eggs in empty cells. If the real queen finds those eggs, she eats them.

▲ Bat Girlfriends

Like human teenagers, female vampire bats hang out in cliques of up to a dozen females. Among the group, each bat will find her own "best friend" to be her companion. These pairs groom each other regularly, and they can even recognize each other's voices.

And Baby Makes Three

Dwarf mongooses live in groups led by a single powerful female and her female descendants. Her mate is second in command, but the third most respected animal in a group of mongooses is Baby—the lead female's youngest offspring.

Going Home to Mother

When it's time for a dolphin to give birth, she returns to her mother's pod to bear and raise her baby. Grandmother dolphins play an important role in a calf's upbringing—they are the ones who teach it where to find food and safety.

The Sisters and the Cousins and the Aunts

Elephants live in a matriarchy—one old female elephant leading a group of up to two dozen daughters, sisters, nieces, and aunts. They have no place in their system for mature males. The sons are kicked out of the family group when they are fully grown—at about age 15.

Girl Power

R-E-S-P-E-C-T
Even the most aggressive male hippo
must be polite when he approaches
a crèche—the group of mothers and
babies that lives in the middle of a
school of hippos. If a female rises,
the male must sit to show his respect.
If he doesn't, all the females in the
crèche will turn and attack him.

first comes

how animal babies come to be

love

She Loves Me, She Loves Me Not
A female leopard seeking a mate will seem
friendly to a male, sharing a kill or rubbing
cheeks with him. But she may turn and
lash out at him with extended claws and a
fearsome snarl. This love-hate relationship
continues until the two have mated, after
which she drives him away.

Looking for Love

Maypole Dance

Bowerbirds are known for building complex structures of sticks, where they dance and woo their mates. But only MacGregor's bowerbird builds a tower. When he is done building, he attracts females by dancing around and around its base as though it were a kind of maypole.

Jumping for Joy

When sandhill cranes do their intricate dance of courtship, they build up to a frenzy of leaping, sometimes jumping as high as 15 feet in the air. This gets the whole flock so excited that all the other cranes start bouncing up and down too.

Flashy Threads

The tragopan pheasant dresses to impress. When he's courting, first he shows the female his silver-spotted crimson feathers. Then he brings the two bright blue fleshy horns on his head straight up and inflates a flap on his chest into a turquoise, teal, and scarlet balloon.

▲ Did I Get Your Attention?

When a male marvelous spatuletail hummingbird of Peru wants a female to notice him, he hovers directly in front of her, waving his long tail feathers like signal flags to show her his interest.

Disco Lights, Disco Nights

In Borneo, male fireflies can blink in rhythm. Soon the mangrove trees where they hover look like huge, pulsating dance floors, visible to any interested females from as far as a quarter of a mile away.

▼ A Hare-Raising Courtship

When a male rabbit meets a female who seems interested in him, he may approach her. But often she'll try to rebuff him, rising up on her back legs to punch him with her forefeet, or even leaping in the air and urinating on him as he runs underneath.

Getting into the Act

Two mating elephants stir up the rest of the herd. The others surround the mating pair, flapping their ears, shaking their heads, urinating, defecating, and trumpeting wildly. This commotion attracts more bull elephants, who then challenge each other for mating rights by chasing and shoving, poking with their tusks, and even waging full-fledged battles.

Looking for Love

◀ I Met Him at the Dance

The great albatrosses of the Southern Hemisphere don't start seeking a mate until they're five years old. Even then, they take several years to pair off, meeting at the same breeding colony season after season to perform elaborate dances together. When they do mate, it's for life, and many pairs see their fiftieth anniversary.

Just an Old-Fashioned Love Song

Each night, the male nightingale calls for a mate with long, complicated songs. Every night, his song gets more elaborate until he finally attracts a female. But once the nightingale gets his nighting*al*, that's it for the singing.

Wallowing in Love

When a bull moose is courting a female, he'll invite her to his wallow, a piece of earth he has diligently prepared by digging a muddy ditch and urinating in it. As he works on his wallow, he will lie down and roll in it. When the female comes to visit, she'll roll in the wallow too if she wants to be his mate.

ODD COUPLES

In both these species	Moms and dads are
Giraffes and walruses	cows and bulls
Rabbits and antelopes	does and bucks
Guinea fowl and peacocks	hens and cocks
Warthogs and pigs	sows and boars

Eels live as adults in the rivers of Europe, but they reproduce in the Sargasso Sea, which lies northeast of the West Indies. When the time comes to head back there, the urge to go is so strong that an eel will slither out of a pond and cross meadows to find a stream that leads to the sea.

▶ Who Am I?

I may be hairless, deaf, blind, and hardly bigger than a dime, but I'm an excellent climber already. I'll be crawling through my mother's fur to a safe place inside her pouch, where I'll be living for the next two months until I'm big enough to venture outside. (Turn page for answer.)

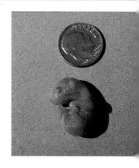

Wild Babies

▼ Great with Child

Elephant pregnancies last for 18 to 22 months, the longest of any mammal's.

I'm an opossum.

▶ Out on a Limb
The fairy tern lays only one egg at a time, on the bare branch of a low bush or tree.

Top Producer
The ocean sunfish lays the most eggs of any fish. A single female may lay as many as 300 million at a time.

A Really Big Family
Madagascar's tailless tenrec, a small insect-eater, carries the largest litter of any mammal. She'll have up to 32 babies at a time, although fewer than 20 will survive.

Egg Heads
Only two mammals in the world lay eggs instead of giving birth—the platypus and the echidna, both from Australia.

A Tremendous Termite
A termite queen may swell so large with eggs that she will grow to be 20 times the size of a worker termite. In some termite species, those bulging queens can lay as many as 30,000 eggs in one day.

The Fab Four
Armadillos are the only mammals who reproduce in litters of four identical babies. After being fertilized, an armadillo egg spontaneously splits into four, creating identical quadruplets.

▶ Who Am I?
Born in the middle of winter, I am only the size of a chipmunk at first. Fortunately, my mother's milk is so rich in fat—20 percent fat compared to human milk's four percent—that in two months, I will be big enough to follow her around. (Turn page for answer.)

Building a Dream House

Penthouse View
Although the harvest mouse lives underground, it hangs its nest high on a cornstalk, where the mother gives birth in a woven globe of shredded leaves. As the babies grow, the nest stretches until eventually the little mice can stick their heads out through gaps in the walls. Then their mother clings to the outer surface of the overcrowded nest to nurse them.

Like a Rock
Not even a grizzly bear can pry a beaver lodge open. With sticks cemented together by thick mud baked in the sun, this home can resist any attack. Beavers are always improving their homes, and over the years, a lodge can become as large as eight feet high and 40 feet across. They may even construct two lodges—one for summer and the other for winter.

I'm a grizzly bear.

▲ Ouch!
An Australian bird called the honey guide lines its nest with hair. In fact, it's so fond of hair that it will yank strands right out of a horse's tail or a human's head.

Knot Now ▶

Africa's weaverbirds build their nests using the same weaving techniques as humans. They even secure the strands of grass with expert half-hitch knots that would make a Boy Scout jealous. And if a bird is dissatisfied with his work, he'll pull it apart and start all over again.

Gimme Shelter

Tent-making bats seek cover from tropical rain in shelters they make from leaves. A male bat and his harem of as many as 20 females will huddle together, their fine white fur well protected by the foliage.

Child Labor

Green tree ants of Australia use their babies to help construct their nests. While teams of adult workers hold two leaves together, other ants rush to the ant nursery to collect some larvae. They bring a grub to the construction site and squeeze it, causing it to squirt silk. The ants then pass the grub back and forth until the silk has glued the leaves together.

▶ Who Am I?

I don't look exactly like my parents right now. I look more like a honey badger, a carnivore that will attack any predator. If they think I'm a honey badger, predators won't want to eat me. I'll get my trademark spots later, when I can take better care of myself. (Turn page for answer.)

▲ Mansion in the Sky

I'm a cheetah.

Bald eagles build nests that are about six feet wide and four feet tall. As the female adds on to it every year, the nest just gets bigger and bigger. One nest in Iowa that crashed to the ground after 40 years of service weighed two tons.

One-Room Apartment

The ruby-throated hummingbird's nest, just one inch high and one inch around, holds two eggs the size of beans. The nest stretches out as the hatchlings grow. By the time the fledglings leave home, it will lie almost flat.

High-Rise Home

Flamingos' nests are towers of mud that climb as high as a foot and a half above the ground. A single egg rests in a gully hollowed out of the top, safe from floods and the hot ground.

Only the Best Construction Materials Used

Cave swiftlets of Southeast Asia build their nests almost entirely from spit. Their saliva comes out in long, white, lace-like strings that harden quickly. The swiftlet spits on a cave wall and draws the strands around, forming a stiff cup of a nest.

Home, Stinky Home

Predators won't find a burrowing owl's eggs. It lines the tunnels to its underground nest with cow dung. Anything sniffing around the tunnel openings will smell only—*eeewww!*

▼ Home Is Where the Heart Is

House wrens can make a nest anywhere, including teapots and old boots. One wren hatched her eggs on the rear axle of a working car. They also weave all kinds of odds and ends into their nests, including nails, pins, and paper clips.

▶ Who Am I?

I was only three inches long when I was born, but I was already disguised by my black mask. In the next few weeks, as my fur grows longer, I'll begin to develop black rings on my bushy tail. (Turn page for answer.)

Egg-cited About Eggs

Saving for a Rainy Day

The water flea lays most of its eggs in summer, when the weather is nice. But when dry spells or long cold snaps threaten its survival, the water flea instead lays the tough winter eggs it has been carrying around in reserve under its shell. These "backup eggs" may then lie dormant in the dirt for years. They will hatch when conditions improve, bringing another generation of fleas to life.

Quiet Down in There!

A gull chick will make little squeaks while still inside the egg. But even before it is hatched, the chick will fall silent if its parent gives an alarm call.

▲ An Evil Stepmother

Along with her own clutch of about seven eggs, a lead female ostrich will incubate eggs laid by minor hens in the ostrich flock. But some of the foster eggs get short shrift. Because she can only successfully hatch about 20 eggs, the hen rolls the extras about three feet out from the nest. None of the rejected eggs are her own.

Bombs Away!

The Caribbean frog climbs a tree, rolls a leaf hanging over water into a tube, and lays her eggs inside. Later, when incubation is complete, the high pressure in the narrow tube makes the hatching eggs explode, shooting the tadpoles into the water.

I'm a raccoon.

A clutch of bobwhite eggs will always hatch at the same time. The eager chicks start tapping the inside of their shells in a steady rhythm about 24 hours before hatching. This regular clicking gets the slower chicks to speed up, so they'll all emerge together.

▶ Who Am I?

I may look like a pink worm now, but soon I'll be as big as my older brother, who still sticks his head in here every once in a while to nurse. The teat I'm sucking gives a totally different solution of milk from the teat where he feeds. (Turn page for answer.)

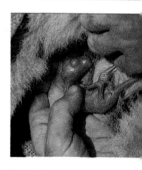

Buggy Babies

Under Your Skin
Caribou serve as the incubators for the eggs of the reindeer warble fly. The fly lays its eggs in the animals' fur, and when the eggs hatch, the larvae burrow into the skin. There they live until they mature into adults, when they drop to the ground, ready to lay eggs of their own.

Feed Me Now!
Yellow jacket larvae are fussy babies. Until they hatch from their cells, they must be kept at a temperature of exactly 86 degrees, which the adults maintain by swelling and deflating their abdomens to create heat. And when the larvae want to eat some chewed-up, pulpy bugs, they let the adults know by scratching at the walls of their cells.

Stocking the Pantry
The ammophilia wasp stuns six caterpillars with her stinger, drags them into a tunnel, then lays an egg on each one. When the larvae hatch, they feast on the captive caterpillars, who remain paralyzed but alive through the entire ordeal.

▲ Snug as a Bug in a Rug

Until a urania moth caterpillar can spin its cocoon, it wraps itself up in a leaf and seals it closed with spit. Then it drags its homemade armor around like a snail shell.

I'm a kangaroo.

I Don't Want to Grow Up
While an immature mayfly lives for more than a year, once it grows up its days are numbered. An adult mayfly survives less than a week, just long enough to find a mate and reproduce.

Born to Be Wild

Right on Schedule
Wildebeests need their babies to be born in time for the great migration season. In any wildebeest herd, between 80 and 90 percent of the calves will be born during one three-week period.

I Could Do This in My Sleep

Black bear cubs are born in January or February while their mother is hibernating. Somehow she manages to wake up just enough to cut the umbilical cord and wash off her tiny, ten-ounce twin cubs. They cuddle up to start nursing from her teats, then the whole crew drifts off to dreamland, waiting for spring and the sun.

A Bumpy Birth

As soon as a baby elephant is born, the mother helps it to its feet by lifting the calf gently with her foot. All the while, she caresses it with her trunk, as if to apologize for the bump on the head it received after falling out of Mom.

Which Way to the Pool?

One poison arrow frog's eggs hatch on the ground. But the mother or father frog immediately whisks its young ones to safety, carrying the tadpoles up a tree to pools of water trapped in the leaves in the forest canopy.

▼ The Jaws of Life

Crocodile babies cry when they are ready to hatch. Mom rushes to the nest, tears open its layers of sun-baked mud, and gently breaks the leathery eggs with her teeth to release the babies. Then they climb into her huge mouth and she carries her brood to the river, where she releases them into the water.

growing up
animal infants

Ahoy, Matey!
Loon chicks sail in style, nestled between
the wings of their mothers as they glide
across a lake.

wild

Born Ready

Ready to Rumble

The first thing a newborn zebra does is learn to walk. It will be able to stand in about ten minutes, can walk well in half an hour, and can canter after 45 minutes. Only after an hour of this testing and trying does a zebra foal begin to nurse.

Claws and Paws

Although newborn lion cubs are almost completely helpless—eyes closed, not even able to walk—their claws are ready for use. They can give a good scratch from the very first day.

▼ Diving for Dinner

Mother hippos spend a lot of their time cooling off in pools of water. Luckily, their babies are designed to nurse underwater. Whenever they suck, their ears fold tight and their nostrils close. While nursing underwater, they just slip to the surface every minute or so, take a breath, then sink back down to continue feeding.

Armed to the Teeth
Spotted hyena cubs are born with teeth. Unfortunately for the mother, they continue to nurse for a full year, even though they begin to eat meat in just three months.

Who Loves You, Baby?

▼ Mark It with a B

In branches high above the rain forest, palm civet mothers mark their babies as their own. While the babies nurse, the mother civet emits a bright orange fluid that thoroughly stains the kittens' fur.

Getting to Know You

After a dolphin is born, the mother and calf will call and whistle to each other over and over again until they learn each other's signature calls.

▼ No, That Jeep Is Not Your Mother

A mother zebra keeps her newborn foal away from the herd for several days until the baby learns to recognize her. Otherwise, it will try to nurse off anything as big as Mom, including gnus or even Land Rovers. Once the foal recognizes its mother's stripes, smell, and voice, the pair will be ready to rejoin the herd.

Distress Call

Baby mice that wander away from their warm nest call out as they get cold. The cries are so high-pitched, only their parents can hear them. That's enough to send Mom out to find her lost children and bring them home.

Oh, It's You

A mother opossum doesn't pay much attention to the newborns that crawl into her pouch. Until they're big enough to climb in and out, she only licks the pouch clean, completely ignoring the dozen or so tiny opossums busily nursing inside.

Who Loves You, Baby?

▼ My Mate Went on a Trip, and All I Got Was This Stupid Rock

As soon as her egg is laid, the female Adélie penguin takes off on a two-week eating binge. The male is left behind to keep the egg warm in the antarctic chill. When the female finally returns, she brings a gift—a stone, which she lays at his feet in offering. Stones, a favorite penguin gift, are used by the birds to build their nests.

A Fussy Father

The malee fowl of southern Australia builds a nest—a hole filled with leaves and covered with sand—where the female buries her eggs. For two months, the male bird continually monitors the nesting conditions, testing the temperature with his tongue. During the warmest part of the day, he pulls some leaves off to cool the nest down. At night he piles the coverings back on.

Heavy Labor

The male sea horse, not the female, gives birth to their babies. The female shoots her eggs into a pouch on his chest, where he fertilizes, then incubates them for two weeks. When it's time to give birth, he will squirt as many as a thousand baby sea horses out of his chest over the course of 24 hours.

Keep That Lip Zipped!

The male Darwin frog incubates eggs in his vocal sac—the big fold of neck skin that swells when he croaks. The eggs hatch as tadpoles and grow into little frogs without ever leaving the sac. The daddy frog doesn't spit them out until their tails have fallen off and they're ready to live on their own.

▶ Role Reversal

Unlike most birds, drab father jaçanas are home tending the eggs while the female birds are out and about, preening their bright, attention-getting feathers and fighting among themselves for the right to control the males' nests.

A Kid's Got to Eat

Oh, Your Breath!
Young elephants learn about the best kinds of plants to eat by putting their trunks in their mother's mouth to smell what she has eaten lately.

▼ Kissy, Kissy
Wolf puppies get excited when an adult enters the den because it means dinner-time. They jump at the adult, biting at its muzzle until the wolf regurgitates some food that they then lick out of its mouth.

Hurry Up, Mom, We're Hungry!
Just one robin chick may eat up to 14 feet worth of worms in one day. This keeps robin parents busy.

Just One More Drink of Water, Please?
There's not a lot to drink where sand grouse nest. They breed in hot, sun-baked areas, so the parents have to carry water in. Mom and Dad bring water back to the nest in their breast feathers, which they soak during their daily drink.

Children First
Large predators that live in groups, such as wolves and lions, usually let the adults eat their fill before any young animal gets a turn. African wild dogs are the only predators who let their pups eat dinner first.

A Side of Fries
The female discus, a fish found in the Amazon River, feeds its fry right off her body. She secretes a rich, nutritious kind of mucus from her sides, which the little fish eat by nibbling on her flanks.

Just a Big Baby
A pilot whale calf may continue to nurse until it is 17 years old.

▼ Hang in There

A nursing baby deer mouse sucks so hard that it will stay attached to its mother even if she jumps up and runs.

No Strollers Needed

Doing Double Duty
A flying lemur needs her gliding membrane—which stretches from the tip of her tail to her ankles—for soaring from tree to tree. But when she's not flying, she can use that skin as a soft pouch for carrying her baby around in.

▼ Give Me Some Room!
Baby opossums climb onto their mother's back for a ride. As many as 17 little opossums must squeeze on whenever the family travels anywhere.

Hey, It's Dark in Here!
A mother panda carries her cub by grabbing its head with her teeth and holding it gently in her mouth.

Get off My Back
Weasel lemurs from Madagascar like riding on their mother's back so much that they won't hop off, even into their own nest.

Belly Up
Mother muskrats use their mouths to carry their babies, grabbing them carefully by the skin of their bellies.

Poisonous Piggyback
Baby scorpions hatch on their mother's back. There they ride out most of their babyhood in safety, sticking close to Mom until they've grown large enough to live independently.

Assigned Seats
When the cubs of sloth bears head out with Mom, each of the two cubs in her litter has a permanent place to ride. One sits on her shoulders, the other on her rump, and they never, ever swap seats.

▼ Let's Play Horsey

Young baboons git along with a giddyup, perched like little jockeys on their mothers' backs.

Protective Parents

▼ Circle of Protection

Mother and father catfish work together to hatch their eggs, fanning and tumbling them with their fins to provide them with needed oxygen. They stick close to the fry when they hatch, too, herding them safely together by swimming circles around them. The young fish can't swim freely until they're at least two inches long.

Was My Face Red!

When an intruder threatens the nest of a blue-and-yellow macaw, the parents furiously defend their chicks. Both the mother and father will scream and fuss at the enemy until their featherless white faces turn bright red with rage.

Open Up and Let Me In

Baby cichlid fish grow up inside their mother's mouth. First she carries the fertilized eggs around, then she keeps the newly hatched babies there until they're big enough to go out and explore. If there's any danger, they swim right back to the safety of her mouth.

Double-Teamed

When a hyena threatens their cubs, mother and father golden jackals will team up to chase it off. First Mom gives it a good bite, and when the hyena turns to attack her, the father jackal bites the intruder's back end. Enough of this back-and-forth bottom biting drives the hyena away, with his backside bent low as he goes.

Fake-Out
If an intruder approaches the hidden
ground nest of a killdeer, the mother bird
tries her best trick. She hops away from
the nest, dragging one wing in the dirt as
if it were broken. She lures the predator
away from her chicks, then—just before
the attacker pounces—she flies off.

Love Bugs

Love Those Kids
Most insects lay their eggs and move on, leaving their young to grow up independently. But the wood roach may take as long as five years to rear one brood of baby bugs.

▼ Chore Time
Roly-polies, or pill bugs, found in many gardens, live in nuclear families, with a father and mother who crawl out into the world to bring food back to their young. After everyone eats, it's time to clean up. The whole family, including kids, carries their pellets of poop out of the burrow.

Dead Meat
Burying beetles start life on a corpse. They hatch on the dead body of a mouse or bird that their parents have dragged into the burrow. As they grow, the young beetles eat the dead animal. But they also beg their parents to squirt some of the regurgitated corpse into their mouths. The parents stay busy tending the corpse, slowing its decay by removing fungi growing on it and coating it with an antibacterial goo they secrete from their stomachs.

▼ Murderous Mother

Baby earwigs spend their first week of life being groomed and tended by their mother. But when the 50 nymphs in the brood molt into their next stage of growth, Mom kicks them out of the nest. And they'd better leave in a hurry. At this stage she doesn't recognize her children, and will eat them if she catches them inside the nest.

An Eggs-traordinary Treat

The subterranean cricket makes sure her little nymphs get enough to eat. As she tends to them in their underground burrow, she'll lay some small, unfertilized eggs now and then. The young insects rush to gobble them down as though they were a delicious treat.

Home Alone

▼ Concealed Weapon

The northern fulmar, a kind of seabird, has chicks that can safely be left unattended, even when the adults must fly 200 miles away to find food. The chicks have a secret weapon to defend themselves from predatory gulls. They save a little oil in their throats from the shellfish they eat, and they can spit it with deadly accuracy—as far as three feet. If the oil hits a gull's feathers, it breaks down the protective waterproof barrier. Next time the gull tries to swim, it will sink.

▶ Looking for a Familiar Face

When 20 million Mexican free-tailed bats give birth in a cave north of San Antonio, Texas, the place is packed with naked baby bats. The mothers leave them on a nursery shelf in one part of the cave and fly out to find food. A mother returning to the cave has to search through a lot of bats to find her child. She crawls over the mass of pups, sniffing and calling. She may screen nearly 2,000 pups until she finds her own.

Baby Snatchers

A female macaque monkey that has lost her baby immediately goes looking for another. Not only is she willing to adopt an orphan, she might even try to kidnap another macaque's child.

Have a Nice Trip, See You Next Fall

When baby raccoons are about five weeks old, their mother leaves them alone in their treetop den while she goes out to eat. While the active babies growl and play, they sometimes get a little too close to the entrance of the den and fall out, tumbling 20 feet or more to the ground. Fortunately, this doesn't really hurt them, and Mom just carries them back into the den when she gets home. When the babies get too active, Mom moves the family to a new den—at ground level.

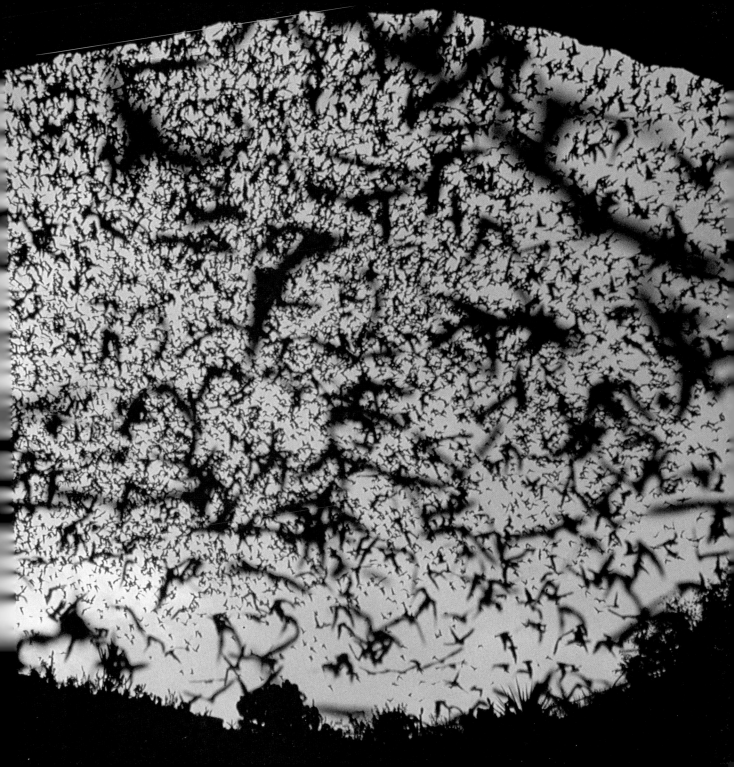

i will sur

when baby grows up

Sea Lion King
Sea lions play king of the hill, taking turns
claiming and being knocked off the top of a
boulder. This builds the skills they'll need
later to fight for, and hold, their territories.

School Days

A Breath of Fresh Air
Manatees, or sea cows, are born underwater, and they have to be taught to come to the surface to breathe. For about a week after her calf is born the mother manatee patiently lifts it to the surface every three or four minutes to get some air. Eventually, it catches on.

Walk This Way

A baby rhesus monkey likes being carried, but sooner or later it must learn to walk. When the time comes, the mother sets it down and walks away. From a distance, she calls to her child, reaches out, and pokes and teases it until the baby stands up and totters over.

Home Schooling

Africa's striped weasels learn to hunt right at the mouth of their den. A mother weasel drags dead mice into the nest until the babies are about three months old. Then she starts leaving half-dead mice outside. She hurries into the nest, noses at her young, and leads them out to the mouse. At first they don't quite get the idea, but after a few days they start biting, tugging, and growling at the mouse, and in two weeks they can hunt for themselves.

Practice Makes Perfect

Young female vervet monkeys who aren't old enough to be mothers spend hours practicing their parenting skills on other monkeys' babies. They're picky, too. They like their charges to be young, no older than three months. And they're social snobs, preferring to play with the babies of higher-ranking females.

A Strict Teacher

When a mother tiger takes her cubs on a supervised hunt to teach them what they need to know, she means business. If they make stupid mistakes or start to get rowdy, she corrects them with a swift slap of a powerful front paw.

▼ Simulated Stalking

Lions give their cubs mock hunting exercises to teach them how to stalk and surround their prey. Later, when the adults go out to hunt for real, they let the cubs know they're not invited. The lionesses' serious, single-minded stride says "grownups only."

Come Out and Play

Cubs Just Wanna Have Fun
Whether wrestling, playing hide-and-seek, or throwing snowballs, bear cub siblings are each other's best playmates. Cubs often continue to stick together even after they're old enough to leave their mother.

You're It

Young peacocks like to play tag. They chase each other around a bush, always running in a counterclockwise direction. The game ends suddenly, with the birds scattering in all directions.

Last One There's a Rotten Egg

Young zebra stallions like to run races. They charge at full speed to an imaginary finish line. Then, when the race is over, they celebrate victory by sniffing and rubbing against each other.

Just a Scratch

Hyenas play so hard when they're young that the cubs end up with big scars from the wrestling and neck biting that goes on in their pretend fights.

Otter Antics

Otters love to drop pebbles, dive and retrieve them, then drop them again. They also may carry a floating object below the water, release it, and chase it to the surface. And they will play with a fish in the same way that a cat plays with a captured mouse, catching and releasing it over and over again.

It's Only Fun Until Someone Gets Hurt

Porcupine siblings practice their defenses in elaborate games, running and dodging, raising their quills, and thrashing their tails at each other.

Playful Parents

Bat-eared foxes never get too old to play. Adults in the wild have been seen playing with sticks with the same enthusiasm as a neighborhood dog.

▼ The Swing Set

A young colobus monkey sometimes uses its mother's tail for a swing.

Leaving the Nest

◀ I'd Rather Be with My Friends

After crocodiles leave home—at about 12 weeks of age—they move in with their peers. A group of young crocs will dig long, deep burrows into a riverbank and hang out there with each other for up to five years.

Come On in, the Water's Fine

Seabirds called murres learn to swim before they fly. Because glaucous gulls would love to eat a murre chick, fledglings make their move from the nest to the sea at night. In the darkness, perched on the edge of a cliff, they fearfully call "wee-loo." Adult males call back from the water below, encouraging them to jump. Eventually, one chick takes the plunge, sliding and rolling into the water, and the rest soon follow.

Temper, Temper

A yearling hyena should be ready to give up nursing, but many of them pitch temper tantrums when they are denied their mothers' milk. An angry adolescent hyena may run around its mother, its lips pulled back in a fearsome snarl, whining and shrieking and complaining. If mother and cub get too angry, they may even bite each other.

▼ When You Just Can't Sit Still

Adolescent springboks can get pretty fidgety. When these African antelopes get really excited, they pronk— bouncing up and down as if they were on a pogo stick, sometimes as high as six feet in the air.

Leaving the Nest

▼ Strutting Their Stuff

Each year, male grouse gather in huge displays of dancing and drumming called leks. A female watches from the center of a circle of strutting birds, choosing the biggest and boldest grouse as her mate. Young grouse start their careers at the outside of the circle. But each year, they get closer and closer to the center, until at last they get a chance to be seen.

Hit the Road, Chick

Japanese paradise flycatchers bribe their chicks to leave home. One bird was seen feeding two chicks that had actually left the nest, as often as 30 times an hour. A third chick, still sitting at home, got nothing.

Lost Youth

The hispid cotton rat of the Carolinas rushes to adulthood. A young rat will be weaned by three weeks of age, and will have her own babies by the time she's two months old.

Just Follow Your Nose

When a bombardier beetle becomes an adult, it seeks out a community of its fellows by sniffing for their odors with its antennae. These beetles must not be too hard to sniff out—their name comes from their ability to fight off attackers by squirting shots of stinky fluid out of their rear ends.

Idle No More

Male fur seals are able to mate by age six, but the big bulls—the "beachmasters"—hold all the territory. The young "idle bulls," as they're called, hang around on the fringes of the seal rookery for four or five years. Eventually they get big and brave enough to battle a "beachmaster" and take over his turf.

▼ Love Conquers All

Around age five, zebra stallions leave the bachelor herds of their adolescence to build their harems. But when a young stallion finds his filly, he'll have to take her against her father's protests—by kidnapping her from the herd.

Index